D1084529

What Is Today's **Weather?**

by Jennifer Boothroyd

first step nonfiction

Lerner Publications Company · Minneapolis

LERNER

SOURCE™

Expand learning beyond the printed book. Download free, complementary educational resources for this book from our website, www.lerneresource.com.

The images in this book are used with the permission of: © JGI/Jamie Grill/Getty Images, p. 4; © iStockphoto.com/BanksPhotos, p. 5; © iStockphoto.com/nycshooter, p. 6; © Kane Skennar/Digital Vision/Thinkstock, p. 7; © monkeybusinessimages/iStock/Thinkstock, p. 8; © XinXin Xing/iStock/Thinkstock, p. 9; © iStockphoto.com/paulaphoto, p. 10; © AlinaMD/iStock/Thinkstock, p. 11; © goikmitl/iStock/Thinkstock, p. 12; © Sergey Borisov/iStock/Thinkstock, p. 13; © iStockphoto.com/sandsun, p. 14; © eduardo_almeida/iStock/Thinkstock, p. 15; © tetra Images - Jamie Grill Photography/Brand X Pictures/Getty Images, p. 16; © Ariel Skelley/Blend Images/Getty Images, p. 17; © Vladimir Voronin/Hemera/Thinkstock, p. 18; © iStockphoto.com/yodaphoto, p. 19; © Jsoe Luis Pelaez Inc/Blend Images/Thinkstock, p. 20; © iStockphoto.com/Rhoberazzi, p. 21; © iStockphoto.com/STEFANOLUNARDI, p. 22.

Front Cover: © iStockphoto.com/Marccophoto.

Main body text set in ITC Avant Garde Gothic Std Medium 21/25.
Typeface provided by Adobe Systems.

Lerner Publications Company
A division of Lerner Publishing Group, Inc.
241 First Avenue North
Minneapolis, MN 55401 USA

For reading levels and more information, look up this title at www.lernerbooks.com.

Library of Congress Cataloging-in-Publication Data

The Cataloging-in-Publication Data for *What Is Today's Weather* is on file at the Library of Congress.
ISBN: 978–1–4677–3916–0 (LB)
ISBN: 978–1–4677–4683–0 (EB)

Manufactured in the United States of America
1 – CG – 7/15/14

Table of Contents

Temperature

What is the weather like today?

Thermometers measure the temperature.

What is the **temperature** outside?

Is it hot?

Is it warm?

Is it cool?

Is it cold?

Clouds and Sun

What does the sky look like?

Is it bright and sunny?

Sometimes the sun gets hidden behind clouds.

Is it partly cloudy?

Do clouds fill the sky?

Fog can make it hard to see.

Does **fog** fill the air?

Look outside. Do you see **precipitation**?

Rain is water that falls in drops.

Is it raining?

Light rain is a sprinkle.
Heavy rain is a downpour.

Some thunderstorms have very little rain.

Rain with thunder and lightning is a thunderstorm.

Hail forms in many sizes.

Hail can form in thunderstorm clouds.

Is it snowing? Short, light snowfalls are flurries.

Long, heavy snowfalls or strong winds with blowing snow are blizzards.

What's your favorite kind of weather?

Glossary

fog – tiny droplets of water floating close to the ground

hail – pieces of ice that fall from clouds

precipitation – forms of water falling from clouds

temperature – the measurement of heat or cold

Index